EDGE
BOOKS

+ INTO THE GREAT OUTDOORS +

FLY FISHING
For Kids

BY TYLER OMOTH

Consultant:
Kevin Jeffrey
Fly Fishing Instructor
International Federation of Fly Fishers

Edge Books are published by Capstone Press,
1710 Roe Crest Drive, North Mankato, Minnesota 56003
www.capstonepub.com

Library of Congress Cataloging-in-Publication Data
Omoth, Tyler.
 Fly fishing for kids / by Tyler Dean Omoth; consultant, Kevin
Jeffrey.
     p. cm. — (Edge books: into the great outdoors)
 Includes bibliographical references and index.
 ISBN 978-1-4296-9902-0 (library binding)
 ISBN 978-1-62065-694-5 (paperback)
 ISBN 978-1-4765-1553-3 (ebook PDF)
1. Fly fishing—Juvenile literature. I. Jeffrey, Kevin. II.
Title.
 SH456.O66 2013
 799.12′4—dc23   2012017693

Editorial Credits
Brenda Haugen, editor; Gene Bentdahl, designer; Eric Gohl, media researcher;
    Kathy McColley, production specialist

Photo Credits
AP Images: North Wind Picture Archives, 7; Bridgeman Art Library: Free
Library, Philadelphia, PA, USA, 6; Capstone Press: Karon Dubke, 19; Corbis:
Ben Blankenburg, cover, Little Blue Wolf Productions, 22, Peter Beck,
27; iStockphotos: Krzysztof Odziomek, 10; Newscom: Danita Delimont
Photography/DanitaDelimont.com/Janell Davidson, 28, Design Pics/Corey
Hochachka, 20, MCT/Dennis Anderson, 4–5; Shutterstock: Dec Hogan, 3,
Dusan Zidar, 11, Gary Boisvert, 26, Korban Schwab, 9, Newton Page, 14, R.S. Jegg, 18,
Sandra Cunningham, 1, 12, Thierry Dagnelie, 16, Timurpix, 24

Printed in the United States of America in Brainerd, Minnesota.
092012   006938BANGS13

TABLE OF CONTENTS

CHAPTER 1

BEFORE THE FIRST CAST

FACT

Salmon can jump up to 6.5 feet (2 meters) high. This ability helps them make their way upstream to lay eggs. It also makes them a lot of fun to catch. A salmon jumping on the line can be quite a show.

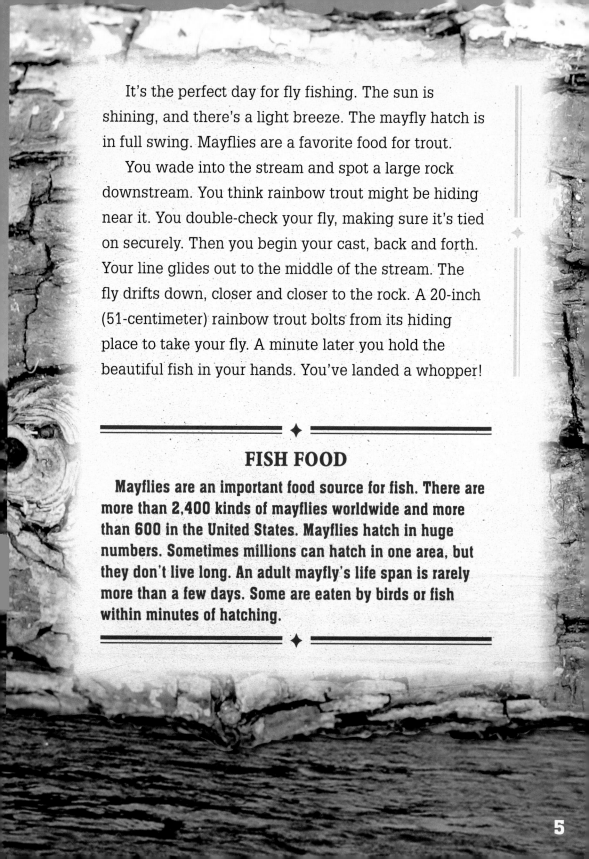

It's the perfect day for fly fishing. The sun is shining, and there's a light breeze. The mayfly hatch is in full swing. Mayflies are a favorite food for trout.

You wade into the stream and spot a large rock downstream. You think rainbow trout might be hiding near it. You double-check your fly, making sure it's tied on securely. Then you begin your cast, back and forth. Your line glides out to the middle of the stream. The fly drifts down, closer and closer to the rock. A 20-inch (51-centimeter) rainbow trout bolts from its hiding place to take your fly. A minute later you hold the beautiful fish in your hands. You've landed a whopper!

FISH FOOD

Mayflies are an important food source for fish. There are more than 2,400 kinds of mayflies worldwide and more than 600 in the United States. Mayflies hatch in huge numbers. Sometimes millions can hatch in one area, but they don't live long. An adult mayfly's life span is rarely more than a few days. Some are eaten by birds or fish within minutes of hatching.

A Long History

Fishing has existed for thousands of years. In ancient times, people made hooks from the bones of animals. They used vines for fishing line and dangled the hooks in the water. Over time, people's fishing techniques became more advanced.

FACT
Pro baseball player Babe Ruth, author Ernest Hemingway, and U.S. President Dwight D. Eisenhower enjoyed fly fishing.

A book written in AD 200 says Macedonians caught fish by making **lures** that looked like flies. That means that fly fishing has been around at least 2,000 years! When European settlers crossed the Atlantic Ocean in the early 1500s, they brought their knowledge of fly fishing to North America.

Today millions of people love to fly fish. You can find them wading in shallow rivers and streams or even casting from a boat on a larger body of water.

lure—a fake bait used in fishing

Types of Fish

When picturing fly fishing, most people think of standing in a stream casting for trout. The trout family includes a wide variety of fish. Steelhead, rainbow, brook, brown, and lake trout are all members of the trout family. You can find trout in rivers, streams, and lakes.

Trout are one of the most popular fish to catch with a fly rod. But there are many other fish that **anglers** can catch by fly fishing. Many fly fishers enjoy trying to catch salmon. These fish are larger than trout and fight hard. Pacific, Atlantic, and landlocked salmon are three common types.

Bluegill, crappie, and yellow perch are smaller fish called panfish. They are common in **freshwater** rivers and lakes. Panfish are not difficult to catch. They are quick to bite and are easily found in open areas. Fly fishing for panfish is a great way to learn the basics of casting and reeling.

angler—a person who fishes

freshwater—water that does not have salt

FACT

Brown trout usually grow larger than brook or rainbow trout. Brown trout can weigh up to 40 pounds (18 kilograms).

rainbow trout

Where you find panfish, you may also find bass and pickerel. These fish eat panfish, and they can be caught with the right flies. Bass and pickerel rarely weigh more than 10 pounds (4.5 kg). Despite their small size, they battle hard. Get one of these on the line, and you'll think you have a much bigger fish.

pickerel

FACT
In 2009 fly fisher Brad Bohen landed a record 51.25-inch (130-cm) muskellunge from the Chippewa River in Wisconsin. That's more than 4 feet (1.2 m) of the toughest freshwater fish in the United States!

bonefish

For those who live or travel to the coasts of the United States, fly fishing can be a fun ocean sport. Many **saltwater** fly fishers enjoy trying to catch bonefish. Averaging between 3 and 4 pounds (1.4 and 1.8 kg), bonefish put up a great fight. If you're looking to hook a really big saltwater fish, try fishing for tarpon. A fully grown tarpon can weigh up to 200 pounds (91 kg).

saltwater—water that has salt in it

CHAPTER 2

GEAR

Fly fishing gear is as interesting as the sport itself. Choose gear to match the type of fishing you will be doing. You also should be sure your line, rod, and flies will work together.

Fly Line

The most important piece of equipment for a fly fisher is the fly line. There are several things to consider before you choose your line.

Your line's density determines whether it will sink or float on top of the water. Floating line is the most common for fly fishing because most insects that fish eat float. Sinking lines go underwater. Sinking lines are most often used in large bodies of water, such as lakes. Sink-tip fly line allows only the end portion of the line to sink. Anglers often use it with **nymphs** and **streamers**.

Taper refers to the shape of the line. Fly fishing line gets thicker or thinner at certain points in the line to create taper. Weight-forward taper adds additional thickness to the end of the fly line, which makes it heavier. This makes casting your line easier. Double-taper line is tapered at both ends. It works well for short-casting in small rivers and streams. Shooting taper line is tapered on one end. It works well for long, smooth casts. Shooting taper line is a good choice for open water such as lakes and for saltwater fly fishing.

nymph—a fly that looks like a young form of an insect

streamer—a fly that acts like a small fish that bigger fish eat

Even the color of fly line is important. During the day, fish can see all lines no matter what color the lines are. Choose a color that is easy for you to see while you fish. For low-light fishing during the evening or night, a dark gray or brown line will blend in with the water.

Backing Line and Leaders

Backing line is line you put on your reel before you add fly line. Backing line is made of a braided material that is strong and flexible. Your reel instructions will tell you how much backing line to use.

A **leader** is attached to the other end of your fly line. The leader is harder for fish to see than the rest of your line. Without a leader, fish would spook away from your fly because of the fishing line connected to it.

Fly Rod

Choose a rod based on the type of fishing you will do. The information attached to each rod in the store will tell you which types of line work best with that rod. A day of fly fishing can mean hundreds of casts. It's important to choose a rod with a weight, thickness, handle, and **action** that are comfortable for you.

Another important feature to consider when choosing a fly fishing rod is its material. Bamboo rods are very good, but they can be costly. Rods made of fiberglass cost less, but they don't cast as well as most other types of rods. Small, powerful graphite rods are a good option for most fly fishers.

Fly Reel

When you hook that big fish, you need a reliable reel to bring it to the net. Choose a reel that works well with your rod. You may also want to change from floating line to sinking line. If that is the case, consider how easy it is to change your reel's spools.

leader—a length of thin line that fly fishers tie to their flies

action—the flexibility of a fishing rod that creates energy for casting when the rod is waved back and forth

wet flies

Flies

All flies are attached to hooks that catch fish as they try to eat your flies. Hooks vary in size according to the type of fish you are trying to catch.

When you get ready to hit the water, you can choose from a huge variety of flies. Flies are made from cork, animal hair, and feathers. Basic flies can be broken down into five main types: dry, wet, streamer, nymphs, and terrestrial.

Dry flies are the most common. They look like live insects floating on top of the water. It's important to keep these flies dry as you fish so they continue to float. Fish see the lure, believe it is an insect, and rise to the surface to strike.

Wet flies sink below the surface of the water. They can look like insects that rise up through the water as well as larger creatures such as crawfish.

Streamer flies look like small fish that bigger fish often eat. Streamer flies act like injured fish to tempt bigger fish into striking.

FACT
Maria Dolores Montesinos Fernandez of Spain holds the record for the longest fly cast into a fish bowl. She hit her target, which was smaller than 7 inches (17.8 cm) around, from 22.96 feet (7 m) away!

Nymphs are flies that are made to look like insects as they leave their eggs. When insects hatch, nymphs rise up through the water to the surface. Using nymphs is a good technique to try when the fish aren't feeding on the surface but are remaining underwater.

Terrestrial flies look like land insects that have accidentally ended up in the water. They are usually larger than standard dry flies. Terrestrial flies can look like living or dead insects.

dry fly

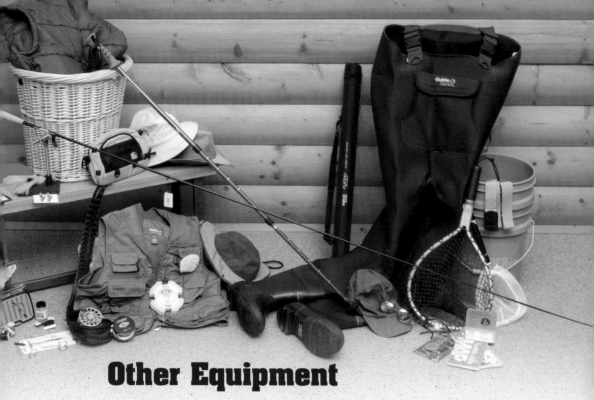

Other Equipment

Once you have your rod and reel set up, it's time to think about the rest of your equipment. Pliers and a fishing net are good tools to keep handy. You may also want a tape measure to measure the fish you catch.

You will often be standing in water when you fly fish. A good pair of knee-high waterproof boots or waders will keep your legs and feet dry. You will also want all your tackle close to you. A fly fisher's vest is a wearable tackle box. A good vest will have a number of strong pockets to hold your fishing gear. Many fly fishers keep flies handy by attaching them to their hats.

CHAPTER 3

TIPS AND TECHNIQUES

You can spend your whole life learning different methods and tricks of fly fishing. The techniques you use should be based on the type of fish you are trying to catch. The area where you are fishing also helps determine the techniques you should use.

Finding the Location

You can't catch fish unless you figure out where the fish are. First, choose the stream, river, lake, or shoreline you'd like to fish. Then you need to study how the water is moving and find the most likely spots for fish to be. This practice is called reading the water.

Slower **current** areas are often hideouts for fish. Fish can rest in these areas because they don't need to fight the current. In a river or stream, look for a bend, rock, or a spot where the running water forms a deeper pool. Also look for ripples on the surface of the water that could signal feeding fish.

In lakes and other still bodies of water, look for weed beds, logs, or **inlets**. Weeds and logs offer good hiding spots for fish. Inlets with moving water are common feeding spots.

Once you've found where you believe the fish are hiding, find your casting spot. The next thing to consider is your presentation. Will you cast directly to the fish or let the current take your fly downstream? If there is a swift current, you may need to let your fly drift toward the fish. Without a current, you can cast right to the spot. You also need a spot that provides plenty of room for casting.

Approach your spot carefully. Fish have good eyesight and startle easily. Make sure your shadow doesn't cross over the water where you believe the fish are. Walk slowly and softly. Avoid splashing the water. Stand still for a while once you've reached your spot. This moment of calm might relax any spooked fish.

current—the movement of water in a river or an ocean
inlet—a narrow bay of water that juts inland

Casting

Casting is the heart of fly fishing. Fly casting takes a lot of practice, but anyone can learn how with a little patience.

Start by making sure you have the right grip. Your hand should be on the rod's grip with your thumb on top. Your thumbnail should face upward. Keeping the proper grip will help your cast be more accurate.

There are two basic motions to your cast: the back cast and forward cast. Start with the back cast first. It's like coiling a spring before releasing its power. Remove any slack from your line before you begin. Holding the line with one hand, lift the rod tip. Then swing the tip back just beyond your shoulder. Your wrist should remain straight. The motion should increase in speed until the moment you stop. The line should unfold in a smooth motion behind you.

Once the rod tip has reached its back-most point, repeat the motion, but forward. Stop just as the rod tip passes your shoulder. Let out a little line, and repeat the process. Watch the rod tip. If it bends straight back and straight forward, the line should fly straight to your target once your release it. After you have made a few casts back and forth, you will have the amount of line that you want flowing. Then lower the rod to your waist during your forward cast, and release the line in a smooth motion.

When a fish surfaces to take your fly, wait for it to turn back down before setting the hook. Fly fishing equipment is more sensitive than other fishing equipment, so don't yank too hard. A slight pull is all you need.

FACT

It is nearly impossible to cast directly into the wind. But that doesn't mean you can't fish on a windy day. If a breeze is blowing, look for shelters or other structures that may block the wind. If you can't find any, look for a spot where you can cast downwind.

EASIEST ISN'T ALWAYS BEST

It's easy to walk downstream and cast ahead of you. However, you'll have a better chance of hooking a fish if you cast upstream from where you stand. The fly will drift down toward the waiting fish. When you pull back, you have a good shot of hooking the fish in the corner of the mouth. That's the ideal hook. The fish will move away from you, making it easier to set the hook.

Anytime you are on a body of water, it can be a dangerous situation. Whether you're in a boat on a big lake or wading in a stream, a little preparation can ensure a fun and safe day of fishing.

The Basics

You might be outdoors fly fishing for hours. That means you'll need to be ready for weather conditions to change quickly. Even on cloudy days, unseen rays of sunlight can be harmful to your skin and eyes. Make sure you have a good pair of sunglasses that block UV light as well as sunscreen for your skin. Polarized sunglasses cut down glare on the water and allow you to see beneath the surface better.

If you're fishing in a river or stream, take special care. If you plan on wading into the water, use a wading stick. A wading stick can help you find deeper holes before you step in them. It can also help you keep your balance as the current sweeps by your legs.

Waders can also be a source of danger. Make sure the top of your waders is at least 1 foot (30.5 cm) above the water line. If your waders are too low, they can fill up with water. The weight of the water in your waders can drag you underneath the water. It's also important to make sure your waders have good-gripping soles so you don't slip on wet rocks.

If you're fishing from a boat, make sure you have the proper boating safety gear. Wear a life jacket. And never stand in the boat to cast. The motion from casting could tip the boat.

FISH HOOK SAFETY

A common injury from fishing comes from fish hooks. If you get hooked, use a pair of pliers to pinch the barb of the hook to make it easier to remove. This also helps you remove hooks quickly and safely from the fish you catch. Always know the location of other anglers before you cast to avoid accidentally hooking them.

CHAPTER 5

CONSERVATION

FACT

Manners are important when fly fishing. Don't fish too close to another angler who has already chosen a spot.

Fly fishing is a sport enjoyed by many anglers in the United States. Everyone needs to pay attention to some basic **conservation** tips to keep the fish populations strong.

Make sure that you are aware of local fishing laws. Never keep more fish than you are supposed to. Only keep fish that are within the acceptable size limits.

Panfish such as sunfish, crappie, and perch can overpopulate a body of water if they are not caught by anglers. Fishing for these plentiful fish is a great way to enjoy fly fishing while helping out the environment.

Pollution is a constant threat to the **habitats** of fish. When you're fly fishing, always pick up after yourself. Don't leave any garbage behind. You should leave your fishing spot just as natural as you found it.

Fly fishing blends the environment with sport. Protecting nature is important to fly fishers. Taking good care of the environment helps anglers make sure their sport can be enjoyed for years to come.

conservation—the protection of animals and plants, as well as the wise use of what we get from nature

habitat—the natural place and conditions in which an animal or plant lives

GLOSSARY

action (AK-shuhn)—the flexibility of a fishing rod that creates energy for casting when the rod is waved back and forth

angler (ANG-glur)—a person who fishes

conservation (kahn-su-VAY-shuhn)—the protection of animals and plants, as well as the wise use of what we get from nature

current (KUHR-uhnt)—the movement of water in a river or an ocean

freshwater (FRESH-wah-tur)—water that does not have salt; most ponds, rivers, lakes, and streams are freshwater

habitat (HAB-uh-tat)—the natural place and conditions in which an animal or plant lives

inlet (IN-let)—a narrow bay of water that juts inland

leader (LEE-duhr)—a length of thin line that fly fishers tie to their flies

lure (LOOR)—a fake bait used in fishing

nymph (NIMF)—a fly that looks like a young form of an insect

saltwater (SAHLT-wah-tur)—water that has salt in it; oceans are saltwater

streamer (STREE-mur)—a fly that acts like a small fish that bigger fish eat

READ MORE

Befus, Tyler. *A Kid's Guide to Fly Tying.* Boulder, Colo.: Johnson Books, 2009.

Crockett, Sally. *Fly Fishing.* Fishing: Tips & Techniques. New York: Rosen Central, 2012.

Schwartz, Tina P. *Fly Fishing.* Reel It In. New York: PowerKids Press, 2012.

INTERNET SITES

FactHound offers a safe, fun way to find Internet sites related to this book. All of the sites on FactHound have been researched by our staff.

Here's all you do:

Visit *www.facthound.com*

Type in this code: 9781429699020

Super-cool stuff!

Check out projects, games and lots more at
www.capstonekids.com

INDEX